Thrive

Spring Outdoor Nature Activities
For Children and Families

The Early Years
2 - 8 years

GW00569977

Gillian Powell M.Ed.

978-1-914225-07-9

Copyright 2021 © Gillian Powell

All intellectual property rights including copyright, design right and publishing rights rest with the author Gillian Powell. No part of this book may be copied, reproduced, stored or transmitted in any way including any written, electronic, recording, or photocopying without written permission of the author. Illustrations and images by the author. Other images used are freely available in the public domain or purchased from stock photography. Published in Ireland by Orla Kelly Publishing.

'It's a wonderous thing how the wild calms a child.'
Unknown

Acknowledgements

Thank you to my husband Tom.

Thank you also to Steve, Dave, Mary, Suzanne, Antony, Philip, Lisa, Conor and Leah.

To Darragh, Dylan and Sophie,and all the little people who made this project special and to all the children and families who have inspired me over the years.

To my wonderful colleagues in early years education, may they be blessed and of course to my wider family and friends.

A special thanks to Liz Casey who gave guidance at all times and of course to Orla Kelly Publishing who made this a lovely experience.

Contents

Spring

Age 2 - 8 years – The Early Years

viii

Introduction

Writing at the turn of the 20th century, Frank Lloyd Wright said 'Study nature, stay close to nature. It will never fail you.' Nature has never failed me. Nature is vital to us and provides delight and surprise, and evidence of everyday miracles in the natural world.

The old clichés ring true, there is the call of the wild,' 'walking the land,' 'I need to get a breath of fresh air.'

Nature is so much a part of sustaining our lives and is vital to us. It is even more vital to children, yet as a result of urbanisation we have raised a generation of children who are in danger of losing a connection to the natural world.

Richard Louv (2005) in his seminal book Last Child in the Woods, refers to a nature deficit disorder. In the past, nature was very convenient for us, and our parents were often outside. We were also sent outside to play. The echo of 'out with ye' ringing in our ears until we got hungry again and came home.

In the modern world, we have to make an effort.

Thrive seeks to help parents and early years educators to enjoy time out of doors, in all weathers, in the garden, in a field, in a forest, at the ocean.

In my thirty-two years as an early years educator in West Cork in Ireland, I have observed that children are happiest out of doors. I have, over the course of that time, developed activities that encourage and enhance children's holistic development. I studied outdoor education as part of a Masters in Education and found that research clearly indicates that trees and natural areas are essential elements of 'healthy communities for communities.' Chalwa (2015).

I would encourage you to step out into a garden, a field, a forest, a beach and engage your child and family in natural activities.

Thrive activities will help you and yours to a sense of emotional, mental and physical health and well-being in the modern world.

Nature also provides excellent opportunities for cognitive development, so pull on the boots and let's explore the forest in Springtime.

What You Need

- ☑ Comfortable clothes and a change of clothes.
- ☑ Waterproof coat – fleece-lined in cold weather.
- ☑ Waterproof pull-ups (fleece-lined), if it is cold.
- ☑ Wellies.
- ☑ Healthy snacks are necessary for any trip with children.
- ☑ Fruit and a sandwich.
- ☑ Water.
- ☑ A flask of tea and a snack for the adults is always a welcome treat.
- ☑ Treasure bag – A special bag to collect the treasures of the walk.
- ☑ Knapsack.

Remember the following

Be safe.

Run free and have
adventures, but make sure
you take care.

Leave no trace.

Be considerate of places
and other people.

It is important to notice things when you go for a walk.

Engage Your Senses

Sight

Prompt questions for children

- Think about the cycle of the day, where is the sun, what time is it?

- Think about the weather.

- Look at the sky, what do the clouds look like?

- Look at eye level, what can you see?

- What colour, shape and size can you see?

- What can you see on the ground?

- Notice the grass, the flowers and every little stone.

Sound

Prompt questions for children

Take a moment to breathe and then listen.

What can you hear?

Bird song, the rustle of the leaves, the gentle breeze or maybe there is more than a gentle breeze.

Touch

Prompt questions for children

What can you feel?

Touch the grass, moss, leaves, twigs, sticks and trees.

For example, can you feel something rough, smooth, prickly or wet?

Sensory Walks in the Forest

What you need.

Go back to page 5

The first moment in the forest is full of excitement, so children like to run and jump and that is great, and after a while, you can integrate learning.

Prompt questions for children

What can you see?

At ground level, you may see twigs and leaves, but you could spot a delicate flower.

At eye level, you may see the sunlight through the leaves, but you could spot a jay bird or blackbird.

At sky level, you will see the tallest tree, but there is a chance of spotting a little red squirrel.

What can you hear?

What can you touch?

What can you smell?

We will explore these questions in the following activities.

Forest Activities

Find a yellow leaf

Find a blue flower

Find a path into the woods

Find a fat twig

Find an insect

Find a tree with a hollow

Find a cloud in the shape of an animal

Find something round

Find a river

Find something that makes a noise

Find a blade of grass

A Nature Scavenger Hunt

Creative activities

Nature Bracelets / Cuffs - Nature Crowns - Nature Leaf Art

(1) Nature Bracelet or cuff

Materials - What You Need

A roll of masking tape, a small scissors, a piece of card to store finished bracelets.

Directions

Cut a piece of tape and roll it sticky side out around your child's wrist.

Roll the tape loosely for comfort and safety reasons.

Children can then pick leaves, flowers and twigs and decorate the bracelet.

(2) Natural Crown

This activity can be extended to include crowns.

Directions

Cut a piece of card to fit and design as desired.

Use masking tape or glue to stick on various treasures from the natural world.

(3) Leaf art

Superhero drawings

Batman or Wonder Woman?

Batman

Wonder Woman

(4) A natural display tree

Create a wonderful tree that can be used throughout the year to display your child's ideas and art.

Directions

Collect different sized sticks.

Make a triangle.

Tie together with light garden wire.

Display on the wall.

Maths Activities

Children love measuring, they love measuring tape and they also love sticks.

If you take a measuring tape to the forest, you can enjoy hours of maths fun.

You can measure the height, width and length of trees, tree stumps leaves and stones.

Extend the learning

This measuring activity can be extended to include numbers and units of measurement.

For example, can you find 5 cm on the measuring tape, and find a stick that is 5 centimetres in length?

Science activities

(1) Potions

Of all the activities that children love doing, creating potions is one of the favourites. Potions can be created with anything in the forest. If there is water - excellent, but if not, mud is a suitable substitute or moss and leaves are just fine too.

You can bring a container of water to the forest in case there is no stream nearby.

Directions

Find a stick.

Collect little bits of moss, leaves, branches and stones.

Add water.

Let the children play with the potions, help them find tiny things in the forest to add to the potion.

What would you like to call your potion?

What would you like your potion to do?

When I asked children in my class of 4-year-olds, what they wanted to call their potion, it was a revelation. There were answers like the 'magic potion' and the 'fairy potion' but there was one child who said 'I want to call it the 'save the world potion." This prompted me to ask 'what would you like your potion to do?,' and the answers were interesting, 'make my Mummy happy,' 'make everyone kind.'

Extend the Learning

(1) Measurements

Creating potions is a great opportunity to explore measurement and recycling. If you have more than one child, each child can carry a container.

Left to right – a biscuit tin, an old cup, 1 litre, 2 litre, and 5 litre containers.

(2) Sticks

Collecting sticks opens up opportunities to examine size and shape. We can describe and explore the concepts of small, smaller, smallest and big, bigger, biggest.

Children can count sticks and group sticks in bundles of 2, 5 and 10.

(3) Stone counting

(4) 5 finger sticks

Counting can include opportunities to write numbers with whiteboard markers.

Complex Learning

Encourage children to create symmetries.

Symmetry – One side of the leaf is a mirror of the other side.

Copying patterns develop 'one to one correspondence' which helps to develop the mathematical brain. (See reference p.38)

Arrange sticks and flowers in a particular order or pattern and ask the child to do the same.

Copy the pattern beneath the line.

References

One to one correspondence refers to the ability of a child to relate an object to its corresponding number.

National Research Council of the National Academies (2009), Mathematics Learning in Early Childhood: Paths towards Excellence and Equity. (P.36) Committee on Early Childhood Mathematics, Christopher T. Cross, Taniesha A. Woods, and Heidi Schweingruber, Editors, Center for education, Division of Behavioural and Social Sciences and Education, Washington, D.C. The National Academic Press.

Language

Language can be extended in all of these activities, but active listening to a child's ideas and engaging with their creative mind, values their play in a sacred way. Perhaps Alexander Fleming, who discovered penicillin started out this way.

The most important aspect of any child's language development is communicating with adults.

(1) Rhyme and Song

Children love rhyme, song and stories. Bring this outside. Families can sit around an imagined camp fire and sing songs and say rhymes.

Baby Shark, one of the most popular rhymes of recent times, can be adapted to Baby Fox.

Songs

A Baby Fox Song (to the tune of Baby Shark).

Squirrel, Baby Bird, Baby Fox.

Baby Fox, doo doo doo doo doo doo,

Baby Fox, doo doo doo doo doo doo,

Baby Fox, doo doo doo doo doo doo,

Baby Fox.

Daddy Fox etc, Mommy Fox etc.

The Understanding of Language

(1) A Visual Game

Children love a treasure hunt of words.

What You Need

1. Make some cards, e.g spotty, thick, thin, stripey.

2. Find objects in the forest that match each card. See the next page.

Directions

Each child chooses a card and finds that object in the forest.

(2) Story Telling

Sticks, Stones and leaves

Who doesn't like storytelling? Sit around in a circle and tell a story. An idea is to get a stone, leaf or stick and to make up the story of that leaf, stone or stick.

Turn-taking can be encouraged by each child who takes a turn holding a stick, stone or leaf.

For example, a child can pretend to be a fairy in the forest – 'I am a fairy and today I am going to visit a bird's nest'.

(3) Literature

I love the word 'literature', from the Latin word letters. There are aeons of memories and generations of learning in literature.

Children's literature is consistently quoted in research as an important way to engage children in learning about the written words.

I have chosen books for you to read with your children that I believe successfully engage young children in both the worlds of literature and the natural world.

The Gruffalo by Julia Donaldson and Axel Scheffler.

The Hungry Caterpillar by Eric Carle.

The Little Seed by Eric Carle.

Owl Babies by Martin Waddell.

And The Good Brown Earth by Kathy Henderson.

The Keeper of Wild Words by Brook Smith.

The Children's Forest by Dawn Casey, Anna Richardson and Helen d'Ascoli.

(4) Films

For a very rainy day, there are two films that engage and delight young children.

Thumbelina (1994) tells the story of a girl the size of a thumb and the swallow that saves her from marriage to a toad. Don Bluth's version is a classic.

The Wind in the Willows (1995) This animated film based on the book by Kenneth Grahame brings the nature to life. 'Spring days my favourite!' Beautifully narrated by Vanessa Redgrave.

Well Being Activities

Finding a Sit Spot.

(1) Meditation

Find a sit spot where you are comfortable anywhere outside and shut your eyes.

Meditation Directions

Breathe in count slowly to 4.

Hold your breath count slowly to 4.

Breathe out count slowly to 4.

Open your eyes slowly like a baby animal, blink gently.

What can you see at ground level?

What can you see at eye level

What can you see at sky level?

(2) Physical Activities

'Keep active, keep alive,' the saying goes and being active is easy in a forest. Find a branch and climb it.

Add a rope and it becomes a brilliant adventure. Climbing a rope really develops core body strength.

In our forest there are 20 fairy doors and children who may be reluctant to go on a long walk, run from fairy door to fairy door. Perhaps your children could create a fairy door trail of their own?

A fairy door trail, could you create one?

Emotional Activities

Children love connection, so remember to connect with them in a positive way during your forest adventure. Reach out and touch their hands. Laugh with them and remember to bring joy to the moment.

Mindfulness Activities

Notice all of the sights, the sounds, the touch, the taste.

This is a beautiful exercise for each child and is best done at the end of each forest visit when everyone is nice and relaxed.

The Sounds

1. Find a sit spot.

2. Close your eyes.

3. Breathe in, count slowly to 4.

4. Breathe out, count slowly to 4.

5. What can you hear?

The Touch

From your sit spot, reach out your hand, feel the ground, feel the moss, the leaves, the bark of a tree.

Feel your own hands.

Gently massage your own hands.

In this moment of gentleness, be grateful for you.

Dear Reader,

If you enjoyed this book, would you kindly post a short review on Amazon or Goodreads? Your feedback will make all the difference to getting the word out about this book.

To leave a review, go to Amazon and type in the book title. Please scroll to the bottom of the page to where it says 'Write a Review' and then submit your review.

Thank you in advance.

If you enjoyed this book, you might also like other books in the Thrive series: Summer - Autumn - Winter collection for the Early years (2 to 8 years).

Lightning Source UK Ltd.
Milton Keynes UK
UKHW020940160421
382084UK00006B/35